The Little CBT Workbook

Other books in the Little Workbooks series

The Little NLP Workbook: A step-by-step guide to achieving personal and professional success

The Little
CBT
Workbook

A step-by-step guide to gaining control of your life

Dr Michael Sinclair and
Dr Belinda Hollingsworth

crimson

The Little CBT Workbook: A step-by-step guide to gaining control of your life

This first edition published in 2012 by Crimson Publishing Ltd
Westminster House
Kew Road
Richmond
Surrey
TW9 2ND

© Crimson Publishing Ltd, 2012

British Library Cataloguing in Publication Data

A catalogue record for this book is available from the British Library

ISBN 978 1 85458 670 4

Designed by Nicki Averill
Typeset by Mac Style, Beverley, East Yorkshire
Printed and bound in Italy by L.E.G.O. S.p.A., Lavis TN

*Dedicated with sincerest gratitude to
our loved ones and to all the clients
we have had the privilege to meet and
work with. Without you, this book
would not have been possible.*

Contents

Foreword

As an occupational physician I frequently see patients who are overwhelmed by the various demands made on them through work, home and life in general. These days we are all bombarded with information via 24-hour television, email and instant global communications. Add to this the uncertainties around job security, worries about the economy and the pressures people feel to 'have it all' and it is easy to see how many of us feel we just can't cope.

Many people see their doctor with symptoms of insomnia, anxiety, tearfulness, loss of control and loss of pleasure in life. They feel unwell and so they seek help from their GP. These symptoms can progress to anxiety or depression if untreated but in the early stages many of these people are not ill but unhappy, overloaded and their ability to cope is exhausted.

Of course, pills are one solution and they can help in the short term, but how do we help people in the longer term? The answer for many is Cognitive Behavioural therapy (CBT): a problem-solving solution aimed at turning negative thinking into positive actions. In the UK, the National Institute for Health and Clinical Excellence (NICE) recommends CBT for the management of many common mental health problems, including depression and anxiety, and with its scientifically proven success rate it's easy to understand why.

CBT is not a quick fix - changing a lifetime of unhelpful habits doesn't happen in a week or two. But many of my patients have come back to see me after completing a course of CBT and said they wished they had done a course when they were 18 instead of waiting until they had become overwhelmed. It has helped them to deal with a range of difficult situations, including relationship problems (both at work and home), and health and sleep problems.

CBT has had a huge surge in popularity over recent years. Partly this is due to cost - most people have six to 12 sessions on a weekly basis rather than much longer courses of other therapies - but it is mainly due to the fact that people see results early on and feel more in control of their lives and better able to cope with multiple demands on their time.

As experienced CBT practitioners and psychologists, Dr Michael Sinclair and Dr Belinda Hollingsworth have helped many patients deal with difficult circumstances and equipped them to cope better with future challenges. As well as helping people in crisis, they offer practical advice on coping and as a result patients are often able to continue in their jobs and maintain a normal routine.

Unfortunately, it is not always possible to start CBT as soon as it becomes evident that a patient needs it. There are often lengthy waiting lists for treatment in the National Health Service and even in the private sector people may sometimes have to wait for a slot to become free. And once patients know that there is help available, understandably they want to get moving as soon as possible. That is where *The Little CBT Workbook* will be invaluable. Patients can familiarise themselves with the theory of CBT and start to practise some of the techniques even before they see a psychologist. They will be in a better position to benefit from formal sessions with their therapist but, most importantly, will feel back in control more quickly.

Dr Sinclair and Dr Hollingsworth have done a tremendous job in making CBT accessible and easy to follow in this very practical book. There is enough explanation of how everyday stressors cause symptoms for the reader to understand what is happening physiologically and psychologically without becoming immersed in too much biochemistry or psychological jargon.

The practical techniques described will help the reader to identify new ways of coping straight away and practice will ensure long-term benefits. By revisiting some of the charts, it is easy to plot progress and see to what extent CBT can alter behaviour in a positive way. Furthermore, this book removes the stigma around common mental health problems and promotes the acceptability of helping ourselves in a healthy way.

Another benefit of this book will be to act as a refresher for people who have already completed a course of CBT. It is only human nature to revert to unhelpful old habits once a crisis has passed and this book will help people to stay on track with positive thoughts and actions.

The book's compact size means it can be easily tucked into a handbag or briefcase. I expect to see many copies being studied on trains and buses in months to come.

Dr Jill Haslehurst, MB ChB DIH AFOM
Occupational Physician

About the authors

Dr Michael Sinclair, CPsychol CSci AFBPsS
As an experienced CBT Practitioner and Registered Psychologist, Michael has provided high-quality psychological treatment to individuals, couples and families for over 12 years. He is an Associate Fellow of the British Psychological Society, a Chartered Scientist registered with the Science Council, and the Lead Clinical Consultant at City Psychology Group, London. Along with his impressive academic background, he has gained extensive experience delivering CBT in GP surgeries, occupational health departments and the Royal Free Hospital, London. He regularly provides CBT training and clinical supervision to other health professionals. He is often sought after in the media as a CBT expert and has published self-help books as well as academic papers on his research.

Dr Belinda Hollingsworth, CPsychol MAPS CCLIN

Belinda is a Chartered Practitioner Psychologist who has been
working with clients within a CBT framework since she began
her postgraduate training in 2006. She is a member of both the
British and Australian Psychological Societies. She currently works
as a senior clinician at City Psychology Group, London. Belinda
regularly utilises her CBT expertise to help people overcome
their challenges and gain an enhanced quality of life. Belinda's
professional opinion has been sought in the media; she has been
interviewed on BBC Radio 5 Live. She is especially proud of this
book as it is her first publication.

Introduction

As you begin reading this book, you may be wondering if it is right for you. What was it that made you pick it up? Perhaps you have heard of CBT and thought it sounded interesting. Perhaps a loved one has had CBT and spoken highly of it. You may have even had some yourself and now want to learn more. Perhaps you feel that things aren't right for you at the moment and you're looking for some help. Alternatively, perhaps, you are happy in your life, but feel there is room for improvement. If any (or all!) of the above relate to you, this book can help. CBT has been considered one of the paramount interventions in the field of psychology for over 30 years and can be very effective.

About this book

The Little CBT Workbook is, of course, predominately a workbook. Therefore our emphasis is on helping you develop practical skills to manage your emotional experiences more effectively in your daily life. Our aim is to provide a comprehensive guide of principles and techniques that can make an immediate impact on your mood and, consequently, your life. Therefore, we are going to provide you with an explanation of CBT 'in a nutshell', which will give you a solid working base to build upon.

How to get the most from the book

There is no quick fix to psychological change. Although CBT offers a range of practical techniques, it is important not to rush through this book when practising them. The techniques are simple but change can be difficult and often takes effort and a lot of patience. We understand that you may want to have a read through this book from beginning to end at first, but bear in mind that the more you pause and practise the techniques and exercises the more you will notice the benefits of CBT. You may find that certain uncomfortable feelings emerge while reading this book, but please don't let this put you off as perseverance is the key.

Authors' notes

Case examples in this book

Case examples have been used in this book to demonstrate the philosophy, tools and techniques of CBT. The authors respect the privacy of each of their clients and therefore this book does not contain any detail of actual clinical cases with whom they have worked. All names, circumstances and identifying markers that resemble real people or events are entirely coincidental and should be considered as such.

The use and scope of this book

Please note that this book and the techniques within it are designed to assist with self-help. This book and its contents are not to be used in the diagnosis or formal treatment of any psychological conditions, nor are they to be used to replace the services of a trained and qualified mental health professional.

Part 1
CBT and you

In this first part of the book, we are going to share the basic principles and philosophy of CBT. Examples and exercises are included, which will help you begin understanding yourself with CBT and notice how it can have a profound impact on your life.

1 How CBT can change your life

We all want to be happy, right? Although we often differ in what our definition of happiness is, it is something that is universally pursued. Most of us have had the thought: 'I would be happy if ...'. The 'if' usually refers to changes in our situation, such as more money, a bigger house, a different job, etc. Given our fixation with pursuing happiness, scientific researchers have dedicated a lot of time trying to uncover the secret to happiness. In fact, people who define themselves as happy and people who define themselves as unhappy have been analysed over the years to try and work out the difference between them: just what is it that makes one group happy and the other group unhappy?

What do you think? Is it that happy people are richer, thinner or healthier? Or is it that happy people have had fewer sad events in their life than unhappy people? Well, the answer may surprise you: statistically speaking happy and unhappy people do not differ *at all* on these points. Happy people are not richer, thinner or healthier than their unhappy counterparts, nor have they experienced less loss or trauma. This means that there is no difference in their life circumstance!

So what is the difference? If our life situation does not determine our feelings, what does? It actually comes down to our perspective or thoughts on our situation.

Is the glass half full or half empty?

Although this is an over used expression, it does get at the heart of what CBT is and how it can dramatically influence your life. The difference between happy people and unhappy people essentially comes down to whether they see the glass of water (or in other words, their life circumstances) as half empty (negatively) or as half full (positively). Let's stop and think about this for a moment. If we accept this analogy, we must also accept that our life situation may not be the only factor to affect our emotions. Still convinced that all you need is a better house, job, relationship to make you happy? Consider the following example.

Two friends, Melanie and Joanna, both have job interviews on the same day. Melanie is feeling very nervous and as though her heart is going to pound out of her chest! In contrast, Joanna is only slightly nervous and is actually a little excited. Although she is aware of an unusual feeling in her chest it is more akin to butterflies than pounding.

These two women are in an identical situation but are experiencing quite different physical and emotional reactions. This is down to one fundamental difference, which has nothing to do with their pending job interview: their perspective.

Melanie's perspective:

I am so nervous! I don't know why I'm bothering with this. They must be interviewing so many people better than me. I have no chance. They are going to pick up all the holes in my previous experience and see that I won't be able to do it. I'll probably just end up embarrassing myself as per usual.

Joanna's perspective:

I really want this job. I think I've prepared well enough to impress them. I hope they haven't noticed my lack of experience in some areas, but if they ask I'll just be honest and tell them how hard I'm willing to work to bridge the gap. I hope this goes well, I'm sure I can do it.

What are your reactions to that? You're probably thinking there must be concrete reasons *why* Joanna feels more confident, but this may not be the case. Let's look at some questions that often arise when discussing the difference in perspectives.

Frequently asked questions

- What if Melanie is actually less qualified for the position than Joanna?

- What if Melanie's financial situation is worse than Joanna's?

- What if Joanna has more experience of the interview process?

- What if Joanna is more prepared for the interview than Melanie?

These questions usually come up in a bid to explain how Joanna is able to be so positive while Melanie is being so negative. Surely if they were in the *exact* same situation there would not be such a difference between their views. Surely Melanie's situation has to be worse than Joanna's! Of course, this line of thought returns to focusing on the actual situation, rather than our thoughts and perspective on it.

In reality, the external circumstances themselves are often irrelevant; it all comes down to how we view them. The thoughts we have are largely independent of the situation. Take Melanie and Joanna: it is clear from their perspective that they both feel that they have gaps in their experience (a potentially bad situation). However, when Melanie considers this point her thought is, *'They will see that I won't be able to do it.'* While Joanna thinks, *'I'm willing to work to bridge the gap'*. It is the same glass of water, but is it half empty or half full?

An important point from this example is that although Joanna had the more optimistic perspective, she still felt nervous. Having a more positive perspective does not mean that you are always going to be overjoyed and happy. People with more positive thoughts still feel sad, angry, frustrated and worried at times. Their positive perspective simply allows them to manage this in a more helpful way that does not make a difficult situation worse.

What is CBT?

CBT refers to two core aspects of our psychology.

1. **Thinking**
   Cognition refers to all of our thoughts, which includes memories, images, words, etc. Everything that goes through our head falls into this category.

2. **Action**
   Behaviour refers to whatever we are doing with our body at any particular moment. Often, when asked what they are doing, people will say *'nothing'*, but this is actually impossible. We are always doing something. Even sitting on the couch staring into space is considered an action.

Now that we have defined the basic elements within CBT, we can look at what this has to do with how we feel. Basically, CBT proposes that the way we feel at any given moment is a direct consequence of what we are thinking. Let's put this into practice now.

Exercise 1.1
Mood inducement

Take a moment to recall a happy event in your life. You can pick anything you like as long as it stands out as a strong and positive moment in your memory. Try to recall specific details such as what happened, what was said, who was there, where it was, how you felt, etc. Make an effort to recreate this event in your mind for at least 30 seconds before continuing reading.

How did you find this? Most people report feeling happier after this exercise; you may even be smiling right now. If you do feel happier than you did before the exercise, ask yourself the following questions.

1. Is your life any different?

2. Are the personal concerns you had at the start of the book resolved?

3. Have you drastically changed what you are doing right now?

Chances are that you answered no to all of these questions. Chances are that absolutely nothing changed in your current life circumstance; yet you noticed a significant improvement in your mood. Why? Because what you were *thinking* about changed. This exercise has demonstrated a core principle of CBT – our thoughts are the driving force behind our emotions.

Ok, so we now know how thoughts and feelings are related to each other, but how does our behaviour link in? Well, let's think about this ...

- Why does someone cry?
  Because they feel sad.

- Why does someone sit on the couch watching television instead of cleaning the house?
  Because they feel unmotivated.

- Why does someone yell and scream?
  Because they feel angry.

When we think about it, it becomes quite obvious that our behaviour is guided by how we feel. Therefore, how we think affects how we feel, which in turn affects how we behave. And in fact, often the way we behave directly reinforces our original thoughts and therefore our feelings once again.

Consider a time when you have been at work and felt unmotivated. A common behavioural reaction to this feeling is procrastination (surfing the internet, phoning a friend, etc). How did engaging in these behaviours affect your motivation to work? Chances are that it actually fuelled your lack of motivation, rather than quenching it. This process is demonstrated in the diagram opposite.

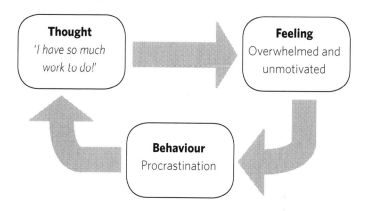

With this example, we can start to see that if we were to think differently about our work, we might feel more optimistic and motivated and therefore more proactive around our work.

So, by using the CBT techniques outlined in the rest of this book, we can target our feelings via changing the way we think and via changing the way we subsequently behave.

2 Understanding yourself with CBT

There is no doubt that there are many day-to-day stressful situations that we encounter, and unfortunately at times we experience other more significant traumatic events. In psychology, we believe that these environmental stressors, albeit very challenging to deal with, actually only serve as the triggers to our distress, and are not the root cause of it.

When we feel stressed, it makes sense that we assume something has stressed us out. We start to look for the cause of that stress: who or what did that to me? We start to assume that our job, relationships, finances or other life situations have caused our stress. However, in doing this we are actually looking too far afield, as the cause of our stress is actually a lot closer than we think!

Difficult situations trigger off our own unique internal response, including thoughts, behaviours and emotions. It is actually the interaction between these that maintains and increases our stressful experience and not the situations around us, as we tend to assume.

Our internal stress response

Psychologists have found there are four 'separate' parts of ourselves in which we have four different types of corresponding reactions or experiences. We experience emotions in our 'emotional-self', thoughts in our 'thinking-self', behaviours in our 'behavioural-self' and physical sensations in our 'physical-self'. It is important to recognise that we don't actually feel emotions in our thinking-self, nor do we have thoughts in our emotional-self and so on. These four separate parts do, however, interact with one another to create our whole psychological experience at any given time.

Let's take a closer look at this interaction now.

Say you were rushing to leave the house whilst running late to catch your train into work in the morning. You might think to yourself (thinking-self), *'I'm so late now, I'm never going to catch that train'*, which may make you feel anxious (emotional-self). This may lead you to start breathing faster and your heart might start racing (physical-self). You may then decide to sit down to compose yourself (behavioural-self). You may then start to think further (thinking-self) *'What am I doing? I'm definitely going to miss that train now and be late for my meeting with the boss!'* This thought may then lead you to feel even more anxious which may lead to even faster breathing and so on. The illustration of the CBT model over the page highlights the interaction between the four parts of us, in all directions.

Interactions that create our experience

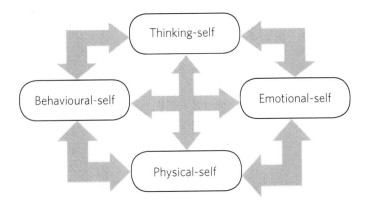

The confidence-cycle

Understanding the CBT model and particularly the interaction between our thoughts and behaviours can shed light on some common experiences reported by people in everyday life.

- How (and why) our stress levels can escalate.

- Why our lives are not moving in the direction we had hoped or planned.

- Why we can be unproductive or procrastinate over our daily chores.

- Why we are fearful of taking a risk, even when we may really want to.

- Why we are lacking our usual enjoyment and zest for life.

It may be that not only do our thoughts (thinking-self) affect the way we feel emotionally but they also have a profound effect on how confident or tolerant we become in the face of our distressing emotions in the future. This effect may not be so obvious to us immediately. Our thinking-self may very subtly be chipping away at our self-confidence over time and it may only be when we notice that we are not moving forward (behavioural-self) that we realise the negative effect it has had on us. Therefore, your thought – feeling – behaviour cycle has both short-term effects (eg how you think, feel and act in a particular moment) and more subtle long-term effects (eg likely to increase or decrease your level of self-confidence) on your psychological well-being.

With the following example, let's take a closer look at this in action.

Say you had a mountain of paperwork piling up and you thought to yourself (thinking-self), *'I can't get through all that, it's just too much!'* Apart from feeling upset (emotional-self), you may also lose some self-confidence as you are thinking about all the things that you *cannot* do. The detrimental effect on your level of self-confidence (albeit usually unknown to you, at the time) will undoubtedly lead to you being more inactive around your paperwork and to put it off some more. You may then have further self-critical thoughts (thinking-self) about your procrastination and lack of motivation, such as, *'What is wrong with me? I'm useless and such a failure, I'll never get this paperwork done now!'* This ongoing self-critical thinking will negatively impact your self-confidence further and so on.

The self-fulfilling prophecy

The vicious cycle of self-critical thinking, self-confidence and behaviour can also help us to understand why we feel anxious about returning to feared situations. For example, we may have experienced some difficult romantic relationships and felt hurt by their ending. We might then avoid new relationships while thinking to ourselves, *'I'm really no good at relationships, I have had two failed marriages, and there must be something wrong with me!'* Such thinking will lead to a lack of self-confidence, which will no doubt lead to further avoidance of situations where you might be able to meet potential new partners, leading to a self-fulfilling prophecy confirming your beliefs about yourself and failings in and around relationships.

Let's face it, if you often think how you have failed at something in the past it will no doubt keep you feeling unconfident to attempt the same or even a similar task again. It could also be said that our self-critical thoughts, along with lowering our self-confidence, are at the same time 'protecting' us, by keeping us away from the emotional discomfort of situations that we don't feel confident enough to manage.

The illustration below highlights the vicious cycle of self-critical thinking, decreased self-confidence and resultant inactivity and avoidant behaviour.

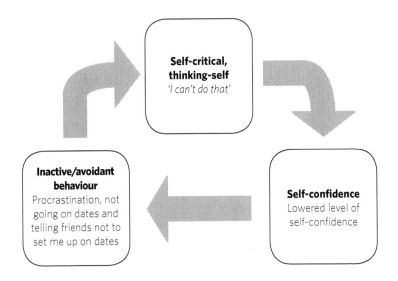

This cycle may help us understand why we have the 'Monday morning blues' and would do anything to stay in our bed when Monday morning arrives, as many of us tend to spend time ruminating about all the things we 'cannot enjoy' or that we 'won't be able to get done' during the working week ahead. Similarly, public speaking or a work presentation is something that many of us dread, as we usually spend time worrying about how we will mess up, fail and embarrass ourselves. Of course, the more we think this way about these situations, the more confidence we lose around them, the more inactive and avoidant around them we will become and the more our thoughts about them become true. Exercise 2.1 will help you to get to grips with your own self-fulfilling prophecies.

Exercise 2.1
My self-fulfilling prophecies

Fill in the worksheet opposite to get a better understanding of your own self-critical thinking and how that might be negatively affecting your self-confidence.

Think of an example where you feel you are not progressing in life or where you avoid a certain situation because you find it uncomfortable. Try to fill in the self-critical thoughts that you may have and the types of inactive or avoidant behaviours that you do as a result of feeling unconfident.

Self-critical, thinking-self

....

....

....

Self-confidence
Lowered level of self-confidence

Inactive/avoidant behaviour

....

....

....

....

Summary of CBT skills

In this first part of the book, we have learnt that it is our thoughts and not the situations, people or events around us that create our feelings. We have also learnt that there is a cyclic interaction between our thoughts, feelings, physical sensations and behaviours that creates our psychological experience and reactions to situations. Furthermore, we have seen how a negative cycle of thoughts, feelings and behaviours can also lower our self-confidence and lead to a self-fulfilling prophecy, often creating the sense that we are not moving forward with certain aspects of life.

Part 2
The 'C' in CBT

In this second part of the book, we are going to take a closer look at one of the two core aspects of psychology that CBT is based upon: our cognitions or thinking. A series of exercises are included to help you understand your thinking and the crucial role that it plays in creating your mood.

3 What is cognition?

You may be wondering why we can't just jump straight into changing your thinking. However, in order to generate lasting change it is important to understand something as it is now: your 'cognition'. Before a mechanic can fix a problem with a car, they need to understand exactly what the problem is, otherwise they will just be blindly re-arranging things under the bonnet, hoping something will click into place.

Cognition is a term that refers to all the mental processes that we use to gain knowledge and understanding of ourselves and the world around us, and our interaction with that world. It includes our thinking, remembering and problem solving skills. Cognition refers to all the mental activity and thoughts we have in our minds.

It is important to realise that thoughts do not just come in words in a sentence structure. They come in all shapes and sizes, such as images, pictures, memories or even sounds. For example, we may think about what we might do today by imagining ourselves via a mental picture of walking in the park or busying away at our desk at work. It is important to remember that our thoughts affect our mood, irrespective of what form they take.

Different styles of thinking

At times, we may notice how our thoughts seem to take on a particular style or pattern. Our thoughts may be focused on the past or the future and they may be positive or negative. For example, we may find ourselves thinking forward to all the relaxing and colourful places we might visit on our upcoming holiday, or we may find that all the horrible meetings coming up at work in the week ahead are running through our mind on a Sunday evening.

When we are stressed or feeling low, anxious or angry, it is often a sign that our thoughts have taken on a negative style and pattern. Our thoughts may be filled with lots of regret about the past or catastrophic projections about what might happen in the future. We may also find that our thoughts contain high expectations for ourselves, others or certain situations and we may find that we are being critical either of ourselves or the world around us.

Sometimes, we can become single-minded and rigid in our thinking, not being able to think fluidly or come up with alternative ways of seeing situations. This is often dependent on how we feel emotionally, as our thinking can take on a 'selective bias' when we feel stressed, low, anxious or angry. For example, imagine that your best friend who had emigrated abroad was now back in town for the week and that you had left a voicemail asking him to call you back but he had not.

Assuming that you feel pretty upbeat and positive, you may not think too much about this and feel assured that he will call you when he has a free moment. Now assuming you feel low and miserable, you may start to question your friendship and think about what you might have done to upset him and how you may never get a chance to enjoy his company again. Of course, the more you think this way, the lower, more miserable and lonelier you will feel.

The diagram opposite illustrates how our thinking may take on a selective bias depending on our mood, and how that thinking will induce more of the same mood, in a vicious cycle.

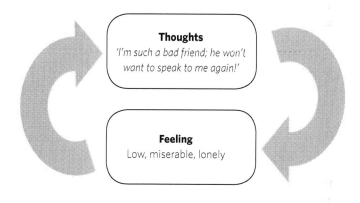

So, the cyclic nature between thoughts and feelings means that if we change our thinking to a more positive outlook we would experience a more positive mood which would result in more positive thinking and so on.

There are often many different ways to think about the same situation. There is never a right or wrong way to think, but in terms of our mood there is always a more helpful and less helpful way to think.

Cognitive workout

It's usual that we will have 'automatic' and immediate thoughts in every situation we face. However, remember that there are always many more possible thoughts and interpretations about each and every one of these moments. For example, in a sad situation, some thoughts will increase our feelings of sadness, while others may allow us to cope with our emotions more effectively. The ability to recognise multiple perspectives in particular situations is called 'cognitive flexibility'. Developing this skill helps people to maintain good psychological health and is a core component of CBT. Try Exercise 3.1 to strengthen your cognitive flexibility.

Exercise 3.1
Cognitive flexibility

Imagine that 100 people are delayed on a train. Each one of these people has their own unique automatic thoughts and reactions to this delay. Now, in the table over the page write down as many different negative and positive reactions to this situation that you can think of. We have included some examples to help you get started.

Negative thoughts

I'll never get to work on time now!

Positive thoughts

Great, now I can read another chapter of this book!

....

....

....

....

....

....

....

....

....

....

....

....

....

....

....

....

This chapter has helped you to gain a better understanding of what cognition is, how our mood can influence our thinking and how that thinking can then go on to strengthen that same mood. You have also seen how there are many different ways to think about the exact same situation by practising your own cognitive flexibility.

4 Identifying your thinking styles

Certain types of thinking styles are known to stress us out, make us feel low, anxious or angry. As we have seen, these thinking styles also often have a detrimental impact on our level of self-confidence. On the next page is a list of common unhelpful thinking styles. Circle Yes if you can recognise any of your own thought patterns in these and provide a short example of when you think this way: for example *'When my partner compliments me'*; *'When I get negative feedback at work'*; or *'When I look at my body in the mirror'*.

Exercise 4.1
Your unhelpful thinking styles

Ruminating/worrying: Going over and over the same thoughts or replaying events in your mind often in a regretful or catastrophic way. It is often circular and obsessive in nature and a definite conclusion is usually not reached, despite spending lots of time pondering.

YES / NO

I use this thinking style when: ....

....

Overanalysing: Excessively questioning events, feelings, behaviours or sensations, often in an endless and sometimes philosophical way.

YES / NO

I use this thinking style when: ....

....

Criticising: Strong negative appraisals of oneself or other people and situations in negatively charged terms.

YES / NO

I use this thinking style when: ....

....

Over-scrutinising: Excessive examination of oneself or other people, often looking for the flaws, mistakes or failures.

YES / NO

I use this thinking style when: ....

....

Blaming: Externalising the root cause of your distress or well-being, thus taking no personal responsibility for either.

YES / NO

I use this thinking style when: ....

....

Our thoughts can contain many unhelpful characteristics, or 'thinking errors', that will undoubtedly lead to negative emotions. Opposite is a list of common thinking errors that many of us use. See how many you recognise and how many sound familiar to your thoughts.

Common thinking errors

All or nothing thinking: When we see things as 'black or white', no shades in between; eg *'I can't even cook a meal, I'm a terrible parent.'*

Over-generalisation: When we take a one-off negative event as evidence of an enduring pattern; eg *'He didn't ring, this always happens to me. No one will ever love me.'*

Mental filter: When we dwell on a single negative detail to the exclusion of all else; eg *'In my job appraisal they said I needed to be more punctual, I must be doing really badly, I'll never get promoted.'*

Disqualifying the positive: When we maintain negative beliefs about ourselves, by discounting positive experiences and compliments from others; eg *'Anyone could have done that, it was nothing special. I can't do anything worthwhile.'*

Shoulds: When we place rigid and absolute demands on events, ourselves and others, not allowing for the natural imperfection of ourselves, others and the world around us; eg *'My partner should know exactly how I feel.'*

Jumping to conclusions: When we draw negative conclusions (often about ourselves) without having the facts to support them. This may be in the form of:

■ **Mind reading:** *'She must think I'm a bit of a loser',* and/or;

■ **Predicting the future:** *'Why take the exam? I'm bound to fail.'*

Magnifying or minimising: When we exaggerate the importance of things (like mistakes or other people's success) and reduce the importance of others (your own positive qualities or someone else's faults); eg *'I really messed that up big time, I'm sure everyone else knew what to do, I'm such a dimwit.'*

Emotional reasoning: When we assume our feelings inform us of facts; eg *'I feel scared and shaky, I'm going to lose control.'*

Labelling and mislabelling: When we describe events in emotionally loaded terms, instead of being descriptive and factual; eg *'What a jerk. He never helps out.'*

Personalisation: When we misattribute personal responsibility solely to ourselves or another when we/they were not primarily responsible; eg *'It's all my/your fault.'*

What thinking errors am I making?

It is important to recognise what thinking errors you may be making to start to relieve yourself of negative emotions. Try Exercise 4.2 to get to grips with your thinking errors.

Exercise 4.2
Identifying your thinking errors

Try to remember some stressful situations that you were recently in. First note the situation and then the negative thoughts that went through your mind in that situation. Finally, try to identify what thinking errors you were making. You may find that you want to refer to the list of common thinking errors on the previous pages to help you label each thinking error you made. We have included an example to help you get started.

Situation: At a friend's dinner party

Negative thought: I'm really quiet, they must all think I'm a really boring person, I should be bubblier, they'll never invite me around again!

Thinking errors: Jumping to conclusions – mind reading; shoulds; over-generalisation; predicting the future

Situation: ....

Negative thought: ....

Thinking errors: ....

Situation: ....

Negative thought: ....

Thinking errors: ....

Situation: ....

Negative thought: ....

Thinking errors: ....

Situation: ....

Negative thought: ....

Thinking errors: ....

Situation: ....

Negative thought: ....

Thinking errors: ....

Situation: ....

Negative thought: ....

Thinking errors: ....

Situation: ....

Negative thought: ....

Thinking errors: ....

Don't be worried if you have discovered that you use unhelpful thinking styles and/or a lot of thinking errors. Most of us engage in some (or all) of these from time to time, so you are certainly not alone! Also, remember that we can only improve on something when we know exactly what we are dealing with. Now that you are better acquainted with your unhelpful cognitive patterns you are in a much better position to change them.

In this chapter you have gained an understanding of the different types of common thinking styles and errors and identified which of these you might usually make. Continue reading to discover how these are affecting you and then how we can address them.

5 Understanding how your thoughts affect you

We often think that the stressful events around us directly cause our negative or upset feelings; but in reality, negative changes in our mood, behaviour and even how we feel physically are actually determined by our perceptions, thoughts and beliefs about such events. So, with some practice, we can identify and change the thoughts that lead to negative feelings and behaviours.

First, it is important to understand how our thoughts are affecting us, which is as easy as **'ABC'**.

The ABC model

A = Activating event

(A stressful event that leads to negative emotions)

Eg Running late to pick the kids up from school

B = Beliefs

(Negative thoughts, assumptions, judgements,
worries, demands on yourself or others)

*Eg 'Other parents will think I'm unreliable and not able to cope for
being late, I am a bad parent, the kids will be upset!'*

C = Consequences

(What is the emotional, behavioural and physical
consequence of thinking this way?)

*Eg Anxiety, anger, rushing, being snappy to the kids, heart racing,
muscular tension, avoiding other parents at school gate.*

The ABC model not only helps to reinforce the causal relationship between beliefs and consequences but also shows us that consequences often strengthen and reinforce our beliefs, further maintaining our emotional discomfort.

Let's practise by putting this ABC model to the test with Exercise 5.1.

Exercise 5.1
Stop, step back and observe

Try to better understand how your thoughts are affecting you emotionally, physically and behaviourally by filling in the A, B and C boxes opposite with a real life example. First identify **'A'**, the activating event and **'C'**, the consequences; **'B'**, your beliefs and thoughts, may not be so obvious to start with.

1. In box A, briefly describe an **activating stressful event** that has occurred to you in the last month.

2. In box C, make a note of the **consequential feelings, behavioural and physical reactions** that you experienced in and around this event.

3. In box B, note the **beliefs** about this event that you think led to this negative outcome.

A

....

....

....

C

....

....

....

B

....

....

....

It is helpful to note also how you would like to react the next time the same or a similar stressful situation occurs. Visualising and noting down your preferred outcome helps you to keep a clearer focus on your goals and strengthens your commitment to change and reach those goals. So answering the following question is very important.

4. How would you prefer to feel and react (emotionally, behaviourally and physically) the next time the same situation occurs?

....

....

By now you will be able to understand how your thinking errors, negative thoughts and beliefs about events are affecting you emotionally, behaviourally and physically. Now let's start changing them!

6 How to change your mood

Changing our thoughts can improve our mood. The best way to do this is to start to challenge our negative thoughts and thinking errors. Let's see this in action.

Activating event
My train is running late for me to get to work

Beliefs (negative thoughts)
People will think I'm unreliable for being late and not able to cope, I'll get into trouble with the boss!

Challenging negative thoughts (alternative, rational thoughts)
I am jumping to conclusions, predicting the future and "mindreading". There is no evidence to say that people will think that way. It's understandable to be flustered when you're running late. My colleagues will understand, in fact I'm often on time and reliable. They may be late too; some of them also get this train. My boss would understand. It's not my fault and if he is annoyed I can talk to him and explain; maybe I could offer to work a bit later.

Emotional consequence
Anxiety and anger

New alternative emotional consequence
Slightly uneasy and frustrated. Calmer and more relaxed. Feeling more able to cope

Challenging negative thoughts

The best way to challenge our negative thoughts and thinking errors is by asking ourselves further questions about them. Here is a list of questions that will help you to start to generate new, more rational and alternative thoughts.

Questions to generate alternative thoughts

- If someone I loved had this thought, what would I tell them?

- Would I be thinking about this differently if I was feeling more positive?

- Am I considering all relevant information (no matter how small!) when forming my view of this situation?

- Am I ignoring any strengths or positives about myself or the situation?

- Am I engaging in any thinking errors at the moment?

- If my negative thought is still true, what is the worst that could happen?

- If someone I trust were to look at this, would they understand the situation differently?

Exercise 6.1
Restructuring your negative thoughts

Try using the questions opposite to challenge your own negative thoughts about one of your own stressful events.

Use the worksheet over the page to help you do this. Notice the changes in how you feel emotionally as a consequence of your new, alternative, more rational thoughts.

You can use the same example you used in Exercise 5.1 if that's helpful.

You may want to do this exercise regularly, or every time you come across a situation you know stimulates negative thoughts.

Activating event ....

Beliefs (negative thoughts) ....

....

Challenging negative thoughts (alternative, rational thoughts)

....

....

....

....

Emotional consequence

....

....

New alternative emotional consequence

....

Keeping my mood in check

It is really helpful to keep a thought and mood diary to ensure that you stay on top of the way you would like to feel emotionally. This gives you a great opportunity to check in with how you are feeling on a daily basis and improves your skills at challenging your negative thoughts.

Exercise 6.2
Thought and mood diary

Take a look at the example diary over the page and try filling it in at least once a day over the next week, to record and attempt to change any unpleasant emotions that you may be feeling.

The diary asks you to do the following.

1. Note the situation that triggered the unpleasant emotion (if this emotion occurred while you were thinking, or daydreaming, simply note that too).

2. Note the automatic negative thoughts associated with the emotion.

3. Record any identified thinking errors and challenge automatic thoughts. You can refer back to the list of common thinking errors on pp.49–51 to assist you. You might also want to refer back to the list of suggested questions to help generate alternative thoughts on p.65–66.

4. Devise more adaptive thoughts to help you change your mood.

5. Rate the intensity of your emotions (0 = a trace and 100 = most intense possible) and your belief in your thoughts (0% = not at all and 100% = completely) before and after you have challenged your negative thoughts.

So, let's start changing our mood!

Example diary

Situation

Who were you with? *Alone*

What were you doing? *Watching telly on the couch*

When was it? *Saturday night*

Where were you? *At home*

Feelings

Describe each mood: *Sad & low*

Rate intensity: 0-100: *85*

Negative thought(s)

Write thought(s) or images (what was going through my mind?):
I am so alone, no friends have called me, there must be something wrong with me

Rate belief in thoughts: 0-100%: *90%*

Thought challenging

Are there any unhelpful thinking styles or errors in my negative thoughts (eg ruminating, all or nothing)? *Personalisation; over-generalisation*

Which technique have I used to help generate alternatives (eg which questions did I ask myself)? *Am I considering all relevant information?*

Adaptive response

Write alternative thoughts to negative thoughts: *I may feel lonely right now but I'm not alone, Sarah did ask me out to the cinema, we could go next week and to that new salsa bar!*

Rate belief in alternative response: 0–100%: *95%*

Outcome

Based on the adaptive response, re-rate belief in negative thought(s): *I am so alone, no friends have called me, there must be something wrong with me: 10%*

Describe and re-rate subsequent emotions: 0–100%: *Low 25%; calm 80%; excited 80%*

Your diary

Situation 1

Who were you with? ....

What were you doing? ....

Where were you? ....

Feelings

Describe each mood: ....

Rate intensity: 0-100: ....

Negative thought(s)

Write thought(s) or images (what was going through my mind?):

....

Rate belief in thoughts: 0-100%: ....

Thought challenging

Are there any unhelpful thinking styles or errors in my negative thoughts (eg ruminating, all or nothing)?

....

Which technique have I used to help generate alternatives (eg which questions did I ask myself)?

....

....

Adaptive response

Write alternative thoughts to negative thoughts: ....

....

Rate belief in alternative response: 0–100%: ....

Outcome

Based on the adaptive response, re-rate belief in negative thought(s):

....

....

Describe and re-rate subsequent emotions: 0–100%: ....

Situation 2

Who were you with? ....

What were you doing? ....

Where were you? ....

Feelings

Describe each mood: ....

Rate intensity: 0-100: ....

Negative thought(s)

Write thought(s) or images (what was going through my mind?):

....

Rate belief in thoughts: 0-100%: ....

Thought challenging

Are there any unhelpful thinking styles or errors in my negative thoughts (eg ruminating, all or nothing)?

....

Which technique have I used to help generate alternatives (eg which questions did I ask myself)?

....

....

Adaptive response

Write alternative thoughts to negative thoughts: ....

....

Rate belief in alternative response: 0–100%: ....

Outcome

Based on the adaptive response, re-rate belief in negative thought(s):

....

....

Describe and re-rate subsequent emotions: 0–100%: ....

Situation 3

Who were you with? ....

What were you doing? ....

Where were you? ....

Feelings

Describe each mood: ....

Rate intensity: 0-100: ....

Negative thought(s)

Write thought(s) or images (what was going through my mind?):

....

Rate belief in thoughts: 0-100%: ....

Thought challenging

Are there any unhelpful thinking styles or errors in my negative thoughts (eg ruminating, all or nothing)?

....

Which technique have I used to help generate alternatives (eg which questions did I ask myself)?

....

....

Adaptive response

Write alternative thoughts to negative thoughts: ....

....

Rate belief in alternative response: 0-100%: ....

Outcome

Based on the adaptive response, re-rate belief in negative thought(s):

....

....

Describe and re-rate subsequent emotions: 0–100%: ....

Situation 4

Who were you with? ....

What were you doing? ....

Where were you? ....

Feelings

Describe each mood: ....

Rate intensity: 0–100: ....

Negative thought(s)

Write thought(s) or images (what was going through my mind?):

....

Rate belief in thoughts: 0–100%: ....

Thought challenging

Are there any unhelpful thinking styles or errors in my negative thoughts (eg ruminating, all or nothing)?

....

Which technique have I used to help generate alternatives (eg which questions did I ask myself)?

....

....

Adaptive response

Write alternative thoughts to negative thoughts: ....

....

Rate belief in alternative response: 0-100%: ....

Outcome

Based on the adaptive response, re-rate belief in negative thought(s):

....

....

Describe and re-rate subsequent emotions: 0-100%: ....

Situation 5

Who were you with? ....

What were you doing? ....

Where were you? ....

Feelings

Describe each mood: ....

Rate intensity: 0-100: ....

Negative thought(s)

Write thought(s) or images (what was going through my mind?):

....

Rate belief in thoughts: 0-100%: ....

Thought challenging

Are there any unhelpful thinking styles or errors in my negative
thoughts (eg ruminating, all or nothing)?

....

Which technique have I used to help generate alternatives
(eg which questions did I ask myself)?

....

....

Adaptive response

Write alternative thoughts to negative thoughts: ....

....

Rate belief in alternative response: 0-100%: ....

Outcome

Based on the adaptive response, re-rate belief in negative thought(s):

....

....

Describe and re-rate subsequent emotions: 0–100%: ....

Situation 6

Who were you with? ....

What were you doing? ....

Where were you? ....

Feelings

Describe each mood: ....

Rate intensity: 0–100: ....

Negative thought(s)

Write thought(s) or images (what was going through my mind?):

....

Rate belief in thoughts: 0–100%: ....

Thought challenging

Are there any unhelpful thinking styles or errors in my negative thoughts (eg ruminating, all or nothing)?

....

Which technique have I used to help generate alternatives (eg which questions did I ask myself)?

....

....

Adaptive response

Write alternative thoughts to negative thoughts: ....

....

Rate belief in alternative response: 0-100%: ....

Outcome

Based on the adaptive response, re-rate belief in negative thought(s):

....

....

Describe and re-rate subsequent emotions: 0–100%: ....

Situation 7

Who were you with? ....

What were you doing? ....

Where were you? ....

Feelings

Describe each mood: ....

Rate intensity: 0–100: ....

Negative thought(s)

Write thought(s) or images (what was going through my mind?):

....

Rate belief in thoughts: 0–100%: ....

Thought challenging

Are there any unhelpful thinking styles or errors in my negative thoughts (eg ruminating, all or nothing)?

....

Which technique have I used to help generate alternatives (eg which questions did I ask myself)?

....

....

Adaptive response

Write alternative thoughts to negative thoughts: ....

....

Rate belief in alternative response: 0-100%: ....

Outcome

Based on the adaptive response, re-rate belief in negative thought(s):

....

....

Describe and re-rate subsequent emotions: 0–100%: ....

Distracting negative thoughts

Sometimes challenging our negative thoughts can be difficult, particularly when the same intrusive thoughts keep popping into our minds. We may find that we are getting caught up in a never-ending loop of alternating thoughts. When this happens it is time to stop trying as we will just be getting ourselves more stressed and losing more self-confidence. Instead we can use a different technique: distraction.

Distracting ourselves from our negative thoughts has two benefits:

1. an often immediate improvement in how we feel
2. an improved level of self-confidence.

When we spend time engaged in negative thoughts, it doesn't feel good, sure, we are making ourselves feel even more distressed, but let's face it, it's not difficult, and doesn't require much effort! What is difficult is trying to distract yourself from these thoughts and focus on them less.

You may find that it feels wrong to challenge or distract yourself from certain negative thoughts because you feel and believe that they are true. However, the goal here is not to determine if the negative thought is true or not, but more how helpful or unhelpful it is to the way you feel.

When trying to distract yourself from negative thoughts it is important to remember what you are trying to achieve: distraction from the thoughts in your thinking-self. Therefore it is no good getting up from the couch and doing some mundane task, like washing the dishes, if you want to distract your mental activity. It is important that you engage in mentally stimulating exercises.

Reading a book, listening to some music or the radio, or talking to someone about something other than what is on your mind are really effective ways to distract yourself. Should these techniques not be working for you, you could try playing some mental games, such as those on the next page.

1. Counting all even numbers backwards from 100.

2. Reciting your times tables or the alphabet.

3. Noticing how many people on the street are wearing blue clothing.

4. Guessing what the people around you might do for a living.

5. Remembering all your past school friends whose surname ends with the letter 'S'.

These are just some ideas but you might be able to come up with some more. The key thing is to distract your thoughts.

Shrinking the problem

It can be easier to distract ourselves when we know that we will have some time to think about our problems later. Knowing that you have some time to let all your negative thoughts run wild can increase the chances that you are able to distract yourself in the present moment. Therefore, you might like to set some time aside in the day, say 30 to 45 minutes, when you allocate time for negative thoughts to run through your mind. It is important to stick to firm time boundaries when doing this exercise and try to distract yourself once again when your allotted time comes to an end. This may sound like a strange thing to do, but it can really help you to gain some control over your thinking and stop your negative thoughts interfering with your whole day.

Summary of CBT skills

In this part of the book, you have understood that cognitions are our thoughts. You have identified what thinking errors you may be making and the negative impact that these errors may be having on the way you feel emotionally, physically and the way you behave. To improve your mood, you have practised challenging and restructuring your negative thoughts as well as different distraction techniques.

Part 3
The 'B' in CBT

So far, we have been focusing on how our thinking patterns can be changed in order to affect our mood. While this is a very effective approach in its own right, when you combine this with changing your behaviour, you can increase your chances of sustaining these positive changes in your mood. So in this part of the book, we are going to take a closer look at the other core component in psychology that CBT is based upon: our behaviour.

Behaviour refers to everything we do with our body and all the actions we take. It is impossible to do nothing, as 'nothing' is still something. At every moment we can identify the behaviour we are engaging in, which of course forms a part of the thought – feeling – behaviour cycle we discussed in Chapter 1 (p.19).

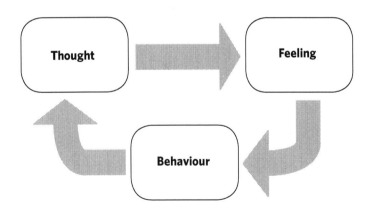

7

'Wellness' behaviours and why you need them

When we talk about 'wellness' we are referring to our psychological well-being. Believe it or not, being 'well' doesn't just happen! Every day, we are engaging in numerous behaviours that help to keep us mentally healthy and resilient without even knowing it!

So which behaviours are wellness ones?

- Eating a healthy, balanced diet.
- Regular physical exercise.
- Enough sleep (eight hours per night is the recommendation).
- Maintaining good physical hygiene.
- Connecting regularly with close friends and family.
- Spending a little time each day outdoors.
- Taking pride (whatever that means for you) in your appearance.
- Maintaining a tidy and clean living environment.
- Taking some time each day for yourself, whether that be reading a chapter of your book or sitting and relaxing on your own.

Of course we are not saying that cleaning your teeth twice a day is enough to keep you mentally well! However, all of your wellness behaviours work together and cumulatively maintain your overall sense of well-being.

It is not unlike spokes in a wheel. Imagine a big wheel with many spokes allowing it to continue rotating. If one spoke is removed, it is likely that the wheel will continue spinning. Even if another spoke is removed the wheel may carry on spinning. However, if spokes keep being removed the wheel will eventually stop spinning and fall. It doesn't stop because any one spoke has been removed but rather the cumulative effect is the factor that stops the wheel turning.

Being well is exactly like the wheel described above. Each spoke refers to one wellness behaviour. If for some reason we remove it from the wheel (eg stop engaging in regular exercise) our wheel may continue to turn, but if more drop off we will find that seemingly out of nowhere our wheel stops spinning and we are left feeling stressed/sad/angry, etc.

Take the following story, for example.

> Brian is a 37-year-old man who works in the City. He
> works hard and also makes time for things he enjoys.
> He is very creative and thoroughly enjoys painting on
> the weekends. He also enjoys running and jogs around
> his local park three times a week. He often socialises
> with friends and goes out on dates now and again.
> He has always felt quite confident and happy within
> himself. However, things changed when a demanding
> project came up at work. Brian found himself getting
> quite stressed and he was finding it difficult to switch
> off and noticed that he wasn't sleeping very well.
> Because he was working consistently late he stopped
> jogging and didn't feel that he had time for painting.
> When he did have time at home he would avoid calls
> from friends and family because he felt too exhausted.
> He would just sit at home in front of the TV, which
> actually didn't make him feel any better. Although
> he was spending lots of time at work he was having
> difficulty concentrating and wasn't being

very productive, which added to his distress. He no longer felt confident in his abilities and was feeling a sense of hopelessness. Brian eventually decided to see a psychologist as he didn't feel able to cope.

Hopefully, this example demonstrates that each spoke in our 'wellness wheel' is helping us to cope more effectively when we come up against difficult and stressful situations. Although Brian did have a demanding project at work, which would generate stress – his behavioural reaction to this actually made the situation worse! In fact, the times when we feel that we don't have time to paint, see a friend or do a workout are often when we need to do it the most! These things allow us to switch off, re-energise and work better.

Exercise 7.1
Spokes in your wellness wheel

Have a think about the spokes that make up your wellness wheel and fill in the worksheet opposite by listing the behaviours that keep you well, in each of the boxes next to the spokes. Include everything that you feel is important to your wellness – regardless of whether you do these regularly at the moment. This is your optimum wellness wheel.

What unique behaviours keep me well?

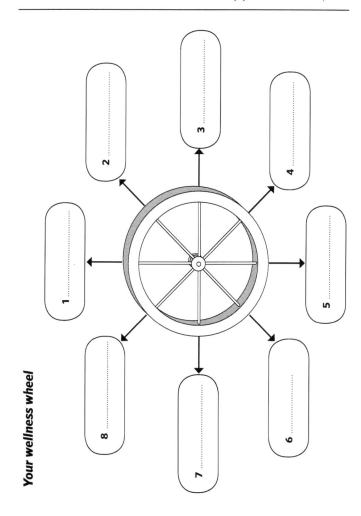

Your wellness wheel

You may find that some of the behaviours you listed have been long gone from your daily life and you feel that your wheel is already missing pieces. Perhaps you feel you don't have time, or don't see them as a priority. Or maybe you feel like you'd really like to change your routine and incorporate more of your wellness behaviours but don't know how. If that's the case, keep reading to learn how.

8 Developing your wellness behaviours

Scheduling your time in a helpful way is a core component of CBT. There are two types of scheduling that we are going to focus on:

1. 'pleasant event scheduling'
2. 'activity scheduling'.

What is pleasant event scheduling?

Pleasant event scheduling is exactly what it sounds like: making time to do things that you enjoy. Doing things that bring us pleasure is an important part of keeping our mood in check. The benefits of doing this not only apply to the specific moment we are doing it, but actually have a more long-lasting effect. People who make time to engage in pleasant behaviours are more resilient and feel more confident in their ability to cope with stressors. On the next page is a list of common pleasant and often relaxing events.

- Socialising with friends
- Gardening, or visiting a garden
- Learning to play an instrument or sing
- Playing with the kids
- Going to the gym
- Treating yourself to a spa
- Watching a funny movie
- Listening to music
- Getting creative, painting or drawing
- Cooking
- Taking a bath
- Reading a book

A common misconception in our society is that spending time relaxing or enjoying ourselves is an indulgence that can only be enjoyed when all the other more important things are done. In fact, many of us feel guilty for taking time purely for ourselves and sometimes even berate ourselves for being so selfish. This is, of course, false; there is lots of scientific evidence that rather than a luxury, 'me time' is in fact a necessity for keeping us mentally refreshed and strong.

Still not convinced? Let's consider the following analogy.

Imagine a large pitcher of water with six glasses.

The water in this pitcher is used to fill the glasses with water. As the owners of each glass take sips, the water in their glass gradually reduces and is continually topped up by the water in the pitcher. Bit by bit the liquid in the pitcher reduces and the pitcher is eventually empty. If we want more water, what do we do?

We simply take the pitcher to its own water source and refill it.

This may seem very obvious but for some reason we don't often apply this logic to ourselves. We are exactly like the pitcher of water! The glasses into which we pour our water (eg energy, time, effort, etc) represent all the areas of our life that we prioritise: family, friends, work, housework, etc. Just like the pitcher, we cannot keep pouring an endless supply of ourselves into these things. After a period of time we need replenishing. Otherwise we are simply going through the motions of 'pouring' ourselves into things, without actually having anything left to give. This can lead to increased stress, burnout and a sense that we are overwhelmed and not doing anything well.

Complete Exercises 8.1, 8.2 and 8.3 to boost your mood through scheduling and engaging in pleasant events.

Exercise 8.1
Identifying your pleasant events

1. Make a list of 10 things that you enjoy doing. You can refer to the list on p.111 for inspiration.

1 ....

2 ....

3 ....

4 ....

5 ....

6 ....

7 ....

8 ....

9 ....

10 ....

2. Consider your diary at regular intervals for the next couple of weeks and commit to doing a few of these activities. You may find that you can fit in more than one over the next week. Write statements indicating which activity you have chosen and when you will do it.

   For example: *To replenish myself this week I am going to have a long, relaxing bath on Wednesday evening after dinner*

   1 ....

   2 ....

   3 ....

Exercise 8.2
Pleasant events diary

For the next week, record your thoughts and your mood before and after engaging in your pleasant events. Over time, this will help you track and prove to yourself the benefits of pleasant event scheduling. Try to fill in the following diary to help with this process.

The diary asks you to do the following.

1. Describe a pleasant event.
2. Record your automatic negative thoughts and emotions about the event, before the event.
3. Record your thoughts and emotions about the event, after the event.
4. Rate the intensity of your emotions (0 = a trace and 100 = most intense possible) and your belief in your thoughts (0% = not at all and 100% = completely) both before and after the event.

Example diary

Date: 07. 08. 12

Pleasant event

Who were you with? Stan and Katie

What were you doing? Going out to dinner

When was it? 7th August

Where were you? In the City

Thought(s) before the event

Write automatic thought(s) or images: I don't want to go. I'm too tired and won't enjoy myself

Rate belief in automatic thoughts: 0–100%: 80%

Feeling(s) before the event

Describe each mood (sad, happy, anxious, excited etc) and rate degree of intensity of each emotion: 0–100: *Fatigued (90); resentful (30); anxious (50)*

Thought(s) after the event

Rate belief in thought before the event: *0%*

Write new thought(s) or images (what was going through my mind now): *I really enjoyed that. It's so good to catch up. It's been worth the effort*

Rate belief in alternative thoughts: 0–100%: *100%*

Feeling(s) after the event

Describe each mood (sad, happy, anxious, excited etc) and rate degree of intensity of each emotion: 0–100: *Contented (100); fatigued (30)*

Date: ....

Pleasant event

Who were you with? ....

What were you doing? ....

When was it? ....

Where were you? ....

Thought(s) before the event

Write automatic thought(s) or images: ....

....

Rate belief in automatic thoughts: 0–100%: ....

Feeling(s) before the event

Describe each mood (sad, happy, anxious, excited etc) and rate degree of intensity of each emotion: 0–100:

....

Thought(s) after the event

Rate belief in thought before the event: ....

Write new thought(s) or images (what was going through my mind):

....

Rate belief in alternative thoughts: 0–100%: ....

Feeling(s) after the event

Describe each mood (sad, happy, anxious, excited etc) and rate degree of intensity of each emotion: 0–100:

....

Date: ....

Pleasant event

Who were you with? ....

What were you doing? ....

When was it? ....

Where were you? ....

Thought(s) before the event

Write automatic thought(s) or images: ....

....

Rate belief in automatic thoughts: 0–100%: ....

Feeling(s) before the event

Describe each mood (sad, happy, anxious, excited etc) and rate degree of intensity of each emotion: 0–100:

....

Thought(s) after the event

Rate belief in thought before the event: ....

Write new thought(s) or images (what was going through my mind):

....

Rate belief in alternative thoughts: 0–100%: ....

Feeling(s) after the event

Describe each mood (sad, happy, anxious, excited etc) and rate degree of intensity of each emotion: 0–100:

....

Date: ....

Pleasant event

Who were you with? ....

What were you doing? ....

When was it? ....

Where were you? ....

Thought(s) before the event

Write automatic thought(s) or images: ....

....

Rate belief in automatic thoughts: 0-100%: ....

Feeling(s) before the event

Describe each mood (sad, happy, anxious, excited etc) and rate degree of intensity of each emotion: 0–100:

....

Thought(s) after the event

Rate belief in thought before the event: ....

Write new thought(s) or images (what was going through my mind):

....

Rate belief in alternative thoughts: 0–100%: ....

Feeling(s) after the event

Describe each mood (sad, happy, anxious, excited etc) and rate degree of intensity of each emotion: 0–100:

....

Date: ....

Pleasant event

Who were you with? ....

What were you doing? ....

When was it? ....

Where were you? ....

Thought(s) before the event

Write automatic thought(s) or images: ....

....

Rate belief in automatic thoughts: 0–100%: ....

Feeling(s) before the event

Describe each mood (sad, happy, anxious, excited etc) and rate
degree of intensity of each emotion: 0–100:

....

Thought(s) after the event

Rate belief in thought before the event: ....

Write new thought(s) or images (what was going through my
mind):

....

Rate belief in alternative thoughts: 0–100%: ....

Feeling(s) after the event

Describe each mood (sad, happy, anxious, excited etc) and rate
degree of intensity of each emotion: 0–100:

....

Date: ....

Pleasant event

Who were you with? ....

What were you doing? ....

When was it? ....

Where were you? ....

Thought(s) before the event

Write automatic thought(s) or images: ....

....

Rate belief in automatic thoughts: 0–100%: ....

Feeling(s) before the event

Describe each mood (sad, happy, anxious, excited etc) and rate
degree of intensity of each emotion: 0–100:

....

Thought(s) after the event

Rate belief in thought before the event: ....

Write new thought(s) or images (what was going through my
mind):

....

Rate belief in alternative thoughts: 0–100%: ....

Feeling(s) after the event

Describe each mood (sad, happy, anxious, excited etc) and rate
degree of intensity of each emotion: 0–100:

....

Date: ....

Pleasant event

Who were you with? ....

What were you doing? ....

When was it? ....

Where were you? ....

Thought(s) before the event

Write automatic thought(s) or images: ....

....

Rate belief in automatic thoughts: 0–100%: ....

Feeling(s) before the event

Describe each mood (sad, happy, anxious, excited etc) and rate degree of intensity of each emotion: 0–100:

....

Thought(s) after the event

Rate belief in thought before the event: ....

Write new thought(s) or images (what was going through my mind):

....

Rate belief in alternative thoughts: 0–100%: ....

Feeling(s) after the event

Describe each mood (sad, happy, anxious, excited etc) and rate degree of intensity of each emotion: 0–100:

....

Date: ....

Pleasant event

Who were you with? ....

What were you doing? ....

When was it? ....

Where were you? ....

Thought(s) before the event

Write automatic thought(s) or images: ....

....

Rate belief in automatic thoughts: 0-100%: ....

Feeling(s) before the event

Describe each mood (sad, happy, anxious, excited etc) and rate degree of intensity of each emotion: 0–100:

....

Thought(s) after the event

Rate belief in thought before the event: ....

Write new thought(s) or images (what was going through my mind):

....

Rate belief in alternative thoughts: 0–100%: ....

Feeling(s) after the event

Describe each mood (sad, happy, anxious, excited etc) and rate degree of intensity of each emotion: 0–100:

....

First act positive, then feel positive

We may not always see an improvement in our mood immediately after engaging in a pleasant event or activity. This is particularly true if our mood has been low or anxious for some time. However, this does not mean that the pleasant events are not working. It simply means that our positive emotions (and perspective) may be so out of practice that they've forgotten how to work! In other words our brain has become so use to feeding our negative perspective and emotions that it has become our default setting. Don't despair if this is the case as persistence is the key. Through engaging in pleasant events (even when we may not want to) we are resetting our mind and re-fuelling our feel-good emotions.

What is activity scheduling?

Activity scheduling is another important part of both improving our mood and minimising stress. It is a crucial element of CBT that directly breaks the vicious cycle that often leaves us feeling stuck in a rut. When we feel low we often feel unmotivated. If we go back to our thought – feeling – behaviour cycle we can see that a lack of motivation, breeds inactivity, which reinforces de-motivating thoughts (eg *I can't be bothered*), which fosters more lack of motivation and so on.

By purposely scheduling activities in your day, you will break this cycle in a positive way! Let's say that you've wanted to sort the growing stack of mail on your desk for several months but haven't felt motivated to do so. If you schedule this into your day and make a commitment to do it, despite any negative thoughts and feelings that you may have, you will increase your motivation and create a new cycle.

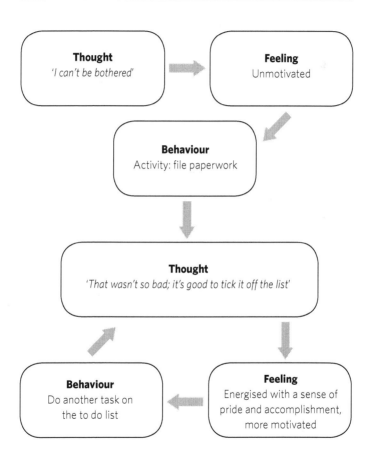

Exercise 8.3

What and when you need to schedule

1. Make a list of 10 things that you want to get done. These may be things that you have been putting off and have a negative or sinking feeling about doing. These can be anything from ongoing projects such as finishing painting the spare room, clearing out the garage etc, to chores and everyday activities such as cleaning the bathroom or replying to correspondence.

1 ....

2 ....

3 ....

4 ....

5 ....

6 ....

7 ....

8 ....

9 ....

10 ....

2. Next prioritise the items in your list. Once you have considered which of these unfinished projects is most pressing, make time in your schedule this week for it. Do not try to do everything at once.

3. Break up the task into specific steps. It is important to make a 'time-oriented' plan rather than a 'task-oriented' plan.

So, instead of committing to 'completely re-organising the wardrobe on Sunday', commit to 'spending an hour (or however long you decide to schedule) reorganising the wardrobe on Sunday'. Sometimes we underestimate how long these tasks take and become disheartened when we can't finish what we started. This could undermine the entire point of activity scheduling and minimise our motivation even further.

You may find that after you've completed your time-oriented task you want to continue with the project. Of course, this is completely fine as long as you remember that after the scheduled time you have completed your goal and anything else is simply a bonus!

4. Spend some time visualising yourself doing the task in your mind and challenge any negative thoughts as they arise (eg I can't, I'll do it later, I don't want to).

5. Now, write a statement indicating which activity you have chosen, when you will do it and how long you will do it for.

....

....

6. On the next page is a sample timetable for you to record which activities you are going to schedule. Writing them down and crossing them off when complete can help generate motivation, a sense of mastery/confidence and increase your level of commitment.

To help with this, the timetable also asks you to rate your sense of achievement for each activity crossed off the list, on a scale from 0–10, where 10 is the most achievement and 0 is none at all. It also asks you to reward yourself for each item you tick of the list to further increase your motivation.

By doing this exercise and targeting your to do list proactively, you can directly influence your feelings in a positive way.

Date (day and time): ....

Activity: ....

Achievement: 0-10: ....

Reward: ....

....

Date (day and time): ....

Activity: ....

Achievement: 0-10: ....

Reward: ....

....

Date (day and time): ....

Activity: ....

Achievement: 0–10: ....

Reward: ....

....

Date (day and time): ....

Activity: ....

Achievement: 0–10: ....

Reward: ....

....

Date (day and time): ....

Activity: ....

Achievement: 0–10: ....

Reward: ....

....

Date (day and time): ....

Activity: ....

Achievement: 0–10: ....

Reward: ....

....

Date (day and time): ....

Activity: ....

Achievement: 0–10: ....

Reward: ....

....

Date (day and time): ....

Activity: ....

Achievement: 0–10: ....

Reward: ....

....

Date (day and time): ....

Activity: ....

Achievement: 0-10: ....

Reward: ....

....

Date (day and time): ....

Activity: ....

Achievement: 0-10: ....

Reward: ....

....

9 Overcoming fear

Master your fears

As we saw in Chapter 2, if you try to avoid situations that make you feel anxious, this can breed a vicious cycle that can often leave you feeling that you are not progressing and not able to enjoy certain aspects of life. For example, if you have a fear of flying this may lead you to feel anxious at the prospect and therefore avoid air travel. This thought – feeling – behaviour cycle is self-fulfilling and reinforcing and ultimately undermines your self-confidence in managing any such distress in the future.

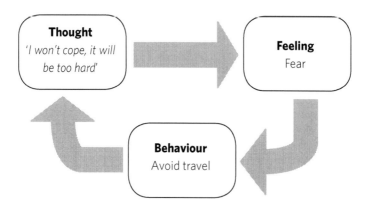

The only way to break this cycle is to put ourselves in the feared situation anyway! At first our anxiety may rise but science tells us that it will always reach a plateau and then fall again. As illustrated opposite, if we continue to put ourselves in this same situation time and again, our anxiety will be less severe and fall a lot sooner time after time.

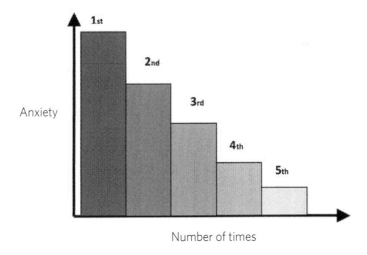

Number of times

Reproduced from Sinclair, Michael, *Fear and Self-Loathing in the City: A guide to keeping sane in the square mile* (Karnac Books, 2010).

'Graded' exposure

The best way to overcome your anxiety in feared situations is to confront your anxiety in those situations gradually over time. It is important to start to confront more minor anxiety-provoking situations first so you can build up your confidence for the more difficult situations. Again it is crucial that you challenge or distract any negative thoughts as they arise, such as *'I can't do it, I won't cope, I'll lose control'*. You should also practise breathing techniques (which we will look at in Chapter 10) in and around these situations. Also don't forget to reward yourself for your achievements.

Exercise 9.1

Conquering your fears

Fill in the feared situations hierarchy on the next page.

1. List the feared situations that you avoid with 1 being the most anxiety-provoking and 10 the least. Be specific when listing these situations. They can be from any aspect of your life: from work to relationships to crowded places.

2. Rate your level of anxiety from 0 to 10, for each avoided situation, where 0 is no anxiety and 10 is most anxiety.

3. Start to confront your anxiety by working up the list from the least to the most anxiety-provoking. Try to confront your anxiety in each situation regularly on a number of occasions before moving up the list. Remember, you are trying to overcome your anxiety so feeling anxious is normal; perseverance is the key.

Feared situations	Anxiety 0-10
1. Presenting in a meeting at work when my manager is present	9
2.	
3.	
4.	
5.	

Feared situations	Anxiety 0-10
6.	
7.	
8.	
9.	
10.	

By working through each item on your feared situations hierarchy list, in a gradual way, you are changing your behaviour from avoiding your anxiety to facing and managing it effectively. This behavioural shift will have a profound impact on the way you think and feel in and around these feared situations. By conquering your fears behaviourally in this way, you will give yourself the unique opportunity to realise that you can manage your anxiety and that you can enjoy more aspects of life again.

10 Take a breath and relax!

Just like making time for pleasant events, it is a necessity for our well-being to make time to relax. Of course it may be possible to kill two birds with one stone if your pleasant event is also something that helps you relax, for example, taking a long hot bath!

However, sometimes we may find that our stress levels are so high that these supposedly relaxing activities don't seem to be doing the trick. Rather than enjoying the warm water and soapy bubbles, we may find ourselves lying in the bath going over all the things we still have to do. When this happens, it's clear our body and mind have forgotten how to relax – therefore we need to retrain them.

Believe it or not, relaxation is actually a skill. It is something that can be practised and learnt. The more you practise, the more you will be able to relax deeply and quickly!

Benefits of relaxation

When incorporated into our daily routines, relaxation strategies are scientifically proved to minimise stress responses, boost your immune system, and create a profound sense of physical and emotional wellness. People who engage regularly in relaxation training usually experience the benefits opposite.

- Feeling calmer in their everyday life.

- Coping with stressful situations more effectively.

- Feeling more energised and clear in their thinking.

- Feeling more confident in their ability to manage emotions.

If any of these things appeal to you, keep reading to find out how you can get there ...

Relaxation training

This chapter outlines two different relaxation exercises. They are both aimed at training your body and mind to relax. Of course practising them both every day would be of great benefit – but we are realists and know how busy life can be. If you commit to the diaphragmatic breathing exercise once a day (it takes less than 5 minutes) and the progressive muscle relaxation exercise once a week you will soon notice great benefits! Before engaging in any relaxation exercise make sure it is safe to do so. You should only do this when you can give it your full attention (eg not when driving, cooking, etc) and when you have not been using any alcohol or drugs.

Diaphragmatic breathing

Although we take breaths automatically, most of us aren't breathing correctly. Most of us breathe through our chest, rather than our diaphragm – which means we are taking shallower breaths.

Secondly, many of us favour either inhaling or exhaling – meaning that our breaths are not evenly spaced and we spend more time breathing in than out or vice versa. Taking shallow, uneven breaths makes us more prone to stress and is the opposite of what we are trying to achieve when practising relaxation.

Exercise 10.1 will help you take steady, even diaphragmatic breaths.

One way to activate your diaphragm is through placing one hand on your stomach, while concentrating on your breath. You should feel your stomach gently rise as you inhale and fall again as you exhale. If you are finding this difficult, it can help to lie on your back.

Once you can feel the rise and fall of your diaphragm you are ready to begin.

Exercise 10.1
Breathing retraining

To begin, simply notice the gentle rise and fall of your stomach as you breathe in and out. Through this exercise we are going to take 10 even, steady breaths.

- Breathe in six-second cycles, breathing in for three seconds and out for three seconds.

- Inhale through the nose and exhale through the mouth.

- As you breathe out, think the word 'relax'.

- Think the instruction below as you practise breathing.

> Breathe in - 2 - 3; breathe out 2 - 3
> repeat 10 times

Don't worry if you find this exercise difficult or a bit uncomfortable at first. It is likely that you haven't been breathing evenly for some time, so it will take practice.

Targeting stress

This technique is also very effective when we are in an acute state of stress. In this case, rate your anxiety from 1 (totally relaxed) to 10 (intense panic) before beginning the exercise. After you have completed 10 breaths, re-evaluate your anxiety. If your rating has not halved (for example, down from an 8 to a 4), repeat the exercise in full until it has reduced. Again, this may take a while the first time you try it, but if you continue practising it will become quicker and easier!

Progressive muscle relaxation (PMR)

Often when we are stressed we are carrying tension in many areas of our body. Common stress spots are shoulders, neck and jaw. However, there may be parts of your body that you haven't even noticed are stressed! We spend so little time focusing on our body that these little aches and pains often go unattended. By simply making time to focus on various parts of the body we can teach tense muscles to relax.

PMR is an exercise in which all parts of the body are focused on individually, tensed for a moment and then deliberately relaxed. Once the body is systematically worked through, a common benefit is a sense of body and mind relaxation.

Exercise 10.2
PMR practice

- To begin, focus all of your attention and energy on your right foot.

- Take a moment to notice if the muscles feel tense or relaxed.

- In a way that is comfortable, tense the muscles in your foot for a few seconds (perhaps by squeezing your toes or pushing them into the floor) and then allow the foot to completely relax.

- Feel all the tension drain into the floor and notice that your foot feels heavy and relaxed.

Follow this same pattern for the rest of your body, in the following order.

1. Right foot (as above)
2. Left foot
3. Left calf
4. Right calf
5. Left thigh
6. Right thigh
7. Lower stomach
8. Chest
9. Left hand
10. Right hand
11. Left arm
12. Right arm
13. Lower back
14. Shoulder blades
15. Neck
16. Head
17. Mouth/jaw
18. Eyes

Please do not strain any part of your body and only move in a way that does not cause pain. Some muscles are harder to focus on than others; this is normal and will improve with practice. Also, some muscles are hard to tense. Simply experiment with ways to tighten a muscle before then allowing it to relax.

Summary of CBT skills

In this part of the book, we have understood how staying well is due to the cumulative effect of engaging in many wellness behaviours. You have seen how engaging in pleasant events, and other activities that you may have been putting off for some time, is the key to breaking negative cycles and increasing your motivation and level of self-confidence. You have also realised that changing your behaviour to facing your anxiety in feared situations rather than avoiding it, is the way to enjoy a more fulfilling life with a greater sense of self-confidence and well-being. Furthermore, you have practised behavioural relaxation techniques such as breathing retraining and progressive muscle relaxation and realised that relaxation is a behavioural skill that reduces stress and increases your overall well-being.

Part 4
What next?

At this stage, you'll have learnt some solid techniques to change your mood. However, this doesn't necessarily mean that you're on 'easy street' from now on in, or will feel incredibly different right away. Working towards changing your moods will come with good and bad days. Just like when we make other changes in our lives such as starting a new diet or quitting smoking, challenges can arise to derail our course. When not dealt with correctly, these challenges can lead to falling off the wagon, which also means that we are at risk of undoing all our progress to date. This section will help you manage common challenges so that even when it's hard, you can dust yourself off and continue on your journey to improving your mood.

11 Overcoming barriers to change

As you may have discovered by now, it is not always easy to change our way of thinking and behaving. Sometimes you may feel unmotivated, defeated or incapable of putting the techniques learnt into practice. You may ask yourself:

- but why is this the case?
- what is it that makes it more difficult on some occasions than others?

Well, if we remember that it is our perception of situations, rather than the situations themselves, that create our feelings the answer becomes obvious: it is our thoughts and beliefs that can make it harder for us to implement change. There are two common cognitive barriers to changing your mood that we are going to look at in this chapter.

1. Resisting change.
2. Questioning negative emotional experiences.

Resisting change

Managing your well-being is no different from maintaining physical fitness – it's a constant work in progress. We may feel overwhelmed with the idea of change and feel a pull towards our old ways. The first thing you need to know is that this is completely normal! Nearly everyone thinks this way at times. So what do we do about it?

We treat negative thoughts about change just as we have learnt to treat other unhelpful thoughts – we challenge or distract ourselves from them. Remember that everything that goes through our minds is a thought and can be treated as such. Go back to Chapter 6 and refresh if you need to.

Exercise 11.1
Interfering thoughts

Below is a list of common thoughts that can interfere with change and maintaining our well-being. Have you experienced any of these thoughts?

■ *'This is too hard'*	YES / NO
■ *'What if I don't get better?'*	YES / NO
■ *'It's not happening quickly enough'*	YES / NO
■ *'What if my thoughts are true?'*	YES / NO
■ *'I don't think I'll ever get there'*	YES / NO
■ *'I don't have time to make new habits'*	YES / NO

Chances are that at least one thought rang true.

But don't despair, remember that each of these can be challenged and restructured; refer to Exercise 6.1 to remind you how. This exercise can be used for any thought that leads to actions inconsistent with wellness behaviours or leads you to fall back on old and unhelpful habits.

Questioning negative emotional experiences

As previously mentioned, many of us focus on situations to explain our feelings, rather than focusing on our thinking and behaviour. Therefore, when we feel sad, angry, stressed, etc we want to find a catalyst; a reason that justifies these unpleasant feelings. Even more than that, we want the reason to be *epic*! Surely something major has to happen for us to feel this bad? Of course, as you've read through this book you will know that this is not always the case. However, we often do find ourselves questioning and sometimes even criticising ourselves when we can't identify a satisfactory reason for our emotions. Perhaps you can relate to one (or more) of the scenarios in Exercise 11.2.

Exercise 11.2
Unexplained emotions

- Feeling a little 'blah' and not able to work out why   YES / NO
- Feeling suddenly tearful and thinking, *'Where did that come from?'*   YES / NO
- Having a sense of dread about an upcoming pleasant event   YES / NO
- Feeling irritable and acting cross with people over little things   YES / NO

Chances are that you have experienced at least one of these in your life; and you may have experienced all of them.

It is quite common when we are feeling a negative emotion to ruminate on the 'why'. It's as though we feel that the emotional experience is only allowed if there is a solid reason for it to be there. This is quite an understandable reaction; however, this thought process usually leads to feelings of anxiety in the short term and lowered self-confidence in the long term. Therefore this thinking is unhelpful.

Emotions do not obey 'rules' whereby they only come out when it's appropriate or justified. Criticising and scrutinising ourselves for not being able to prevent or control our feelings will only increase our negative emotion and lengthen the duration of our upset.

If we do not use CBT techniques to manage the thoughts below, in addition to feeling worse, we will also be more likely to drop our wellness behaviours, which of course will perpetuate the problem.

> - *'Why do I feel this way?'*
> - *'This means I'm really struggling and something is wrong'*
> - *'Why can't I manage like everyone else?'*
> - *'I must be getting worse again'*

Emotions change! We cannot always be happy – and being unhappy at times is a normal part of life. As described in Chapter 7, we don't require a massive event for our emotions to go downhill. If a number of small things change in our behaviours (for example poor sleep, poor exercise, or no time for relaxation) and/or our cognitions/ thoughts (for example over-analysing, ruminating, self-criticising, etc) we can experience a *big* emotional change.

Therefore thoughts focused on 'why' and 'what is wrong?' need to be restructured or distracted from, and wellness behaviours resumed. This may not always lead us to instant happiness, but it will certainly stop us spiralling into sadness or despair.

If you notice that any of these thoughts are going around in your mind, now is the perfect time to go back to Chapter 6 and work through the exercises on challenging and restructuring unhelpful thoughts. Practising these skills regularly will give you a better idea of how to apply them in your daily life.

12 Your well-being MOT

We encourage you to look after your psychological health in much the same way that you might check your car in for an MOT at regular intervals to prevent a breakdown. Making a commitment to practise cognitive and behavioural techniques regularly, even when you are not feeling stressed, is the best way to keep the frequency and intensity of stressful times at bay.

Remember, there is no such thing as pure and constant happiness; that is 'perfection' and therefore an unobtainable illusion. Keep this in mind when you are practising cognitive and behavioural techniques. The human emotional experience is full of ups and downs. Whatever we might be going through, it is normal for our mood to fluctuate – it is what our emotional-self does, that's just how it is!

Therefore improvements in our mood are not just linear in nature; we won't just start feeling a bit better each day. Keep this in mind when checking in with how you feel, as a lot of our distress is simply made worse by the high expectations we hold for ourselves around how we think we should be feeling. It's all too easy to feel depressed about being depressed or anxious about feeling anxious! Learning to accept that you will experience unpleasant feelings at times is the most important key to well-being.

Exercise 12.1
Checking in with yourself

Make a commitment to spend some time each day checking in with your thoughts and behaviours to see if they are in line with your goal of well-being. Ask yourself the following questions.

1. How helpful has my thinking been today?
2. How helpful have my behaviours been today?
3. How would I rate my mood today? (0 = very low and 10 = pure happiness.)
4. What might I like to try to do differently tomorrow?

It may be helpful to record your responses to these questions so that you can have a broader look at how you're making use of CBT techniques. If you notice that you are consistently rating your mood between 0 and 3, you may be experiencing a depressed mood and should consult with your GP and/or a trained mental health professional.

Catch it early!

How often do we hear people talk about their various physical ailments with optimism when the problem has been caught early? This optimism is down to the assumption that it will be easier to treat, which of course is often the case! Mental well-being is no different from physical well-being; when we recognise a problem early the symptoms are less debilitating, the treatment is simpler and the recovery is quicker.

Generally, with psychological health, symptoms simply become larger in intensity and number when they remain untreated. The easiest way to keep on track with your mental well-being is to know what your early warning signs of distress are and to address the problem at this point, rather than waiting for things to worsen.

Exercise 12.2

Early warning signs of distress

On the next page is a list of common warning signs of distress. Everyone is different and some of these will not apply to you. Take a moment to consider each item on the list and see if they represent your experiences of distress. There are also some blank spaces for you to record any of your own early warning signs that are not listed. You may like to ask close family and friends who may notice changes in your behaviour which you had not considered.

Reviewing your list monthly will help you keep track of your psychological state. This will give you a better chance of being able to nip any problems in the bud before they escalate into larger, longer term problems.

Put a ✓ in either the Yes or No box for each item.

Early warning signs of distress	Yes	No
I'm more pessimistic about my life circumstance		
I don't enjoy things as I usually would		
My self-confidence has decreased		
I am more critical of myself		
I cry more than usual		
I feel more agitated than usual		
I lose interest in people and activities		
I find it more difficult to make decisions		
I have less energy than usual		
My sleep pattern has changed		

Early warning signs of distress	Yes	No
My appetite has changed		
I have difficulty with my concentration		
I lose interest in sex		
My body is 'on edge' (eg heart racing, tense muscles)		
I find it more difficult to relax		
I feel more scared than usual		
I avoid my friends and socialising		
I drink more alcohol		
I smoke more cigarettes		
I am snappy and argue more with other people		

If two or more of your early warning signs are present when you reflect on your list every month it's time to engage more fully in cognitive behavioural techniques.

Final thoughts

We thought that now would be a good time to ask you to once again consider what the difference is between happy people and unhappy people. Is it their house, car, figure or how much money they have in the bank? No – it is their perspective on their situation rather than the situation itself! Basically it all comes back to whether the glass is half empty or half full.

With this *Little Workbook* we have brought you the most fundamental and crucial aspects and techniques of CBT, to help you realise them and their benefits straight away in your everyday life.

We hope that this book continues to be instrumental in helping you manage your mood and staying psychologically well. Remember, the CBT techniques included in this book are not a quick fix to any problems that you might be experiencing but instead promote a way of being, going forward in your life.

Practise the techniques and do the exercises regularly, and incorporate them into your everyday schedule. If you do so, we are sure you will notice the benefits of CBT. We wish you the best of luck with your journey to improving and maintaining your well-being!

Here are some of our thoughts on CBT which will hopefully serve as an inspiration to you.

- We cannot control or prevent the undesirable events around us or within us, but we can manage ourselves in relation to such events; in doing so we promote our confidence and well-being.

- Our single-minded pursuit of happiness will result in disappointment, frustration and sadness each and every time; trying to accept the varied spectrum of our emotional experience is the road to well-being.

- Try to ask 'why?' of your experience less; such questioning undermines our confidence, leading to a greater sense of inadequacy and stagnation! The cause of our distress is not to be found in the *answer* to the question 'why?' but is in fact found in the unhelpful (albeit intuitive) *asking* of the question 'why?' itself!

- Pointing your finger in blame is ultimately being self-critical as to do so is to confirm a sense of helplessness, inadequacy and lack of confidence around your ability to change your own reality!

- Perfection is an unobtainable illusion, so there is no point in striving to find it; we never will! Accepting our incompleteness and fallibility is to be complete and full of well-being.

- Try not to make what is uncertain certain: the more you fear something the more it will bite you in the bum!

Further reading and resources

Further reading on CBT

- Branch, Rhena, & Wilson, Rob, *Cognitive Behavioural Therapy for Dummies* 2nd Edition (John Wiley & Sons, 2010)
- Briers, Stephen, *Brilliant Cognitive Behavioural Therapy: How to Use CBT to Improve Your Mind and Your Life* (Pearson Education Limited, 2009)
- Dryden, Windy, *Teach Yourself to be Your Own CBT Therapist* (Hodder Education, 2011)
- Greenberger, Dennis, & Padesky, Christine, *Mind Over Mood: Change How You Feel By Changing The Way You Think* (Guilford Press, 1995)

- Powell, Trevor, *The Mental Health Handbook: The Cognitive Behavioural Therapy: A Cognitive Behavioural Approach* 3rd Edition (Speechmark Publishing Ltd, 2009)
- Sinclair, Michael, *Fear and Self-Loathing in the City: A Guide to Keeping Sane in the Square Mile* (Karnac Books, 2010)

Useful websites

- Alcoholics Anonymous: www.alcoholics-anonymous.org.uk
- Beating the Blues: www.beatingtheblues.co.uk
- British Association for Behavioural and Cognitive Psychotherapies: www.babcp.com
- British Psychological Society: www.bps.org.uk
- City Psychology Group: www.citypsychology.com
- Health Professions Council: www.hpc-uk.org
- Mind: www.mind.org.uk
- Narcotics Anonymous: www.ukna.org
- NHS Choices: www.nhs.uk/conditions/cognitive-behavioural-therapy
- Samaritans: www.samaritans.org
- SupportLine: www.supportline.org.uk